HEINEMANN GUIDED READERS

ELEMENTARY LEVEL

Series Editor: John Milne

The Heinemann Guided Readers provide a choice of enjoyable reading material for learners of English. The series is published at four levels. At *Elementary Level*, the control of content and language has the following main features:

Information Control Stories at elementary level have straightforward plots and a restricted number of main characters. Information which is vital to the understanding of the story is clearly presented and repeated when necessary. Difficult allusion and metaphor are avoided and cultural backgrounds are made explicit.

Structure Control Students will meet those grammatical features which they have already been taught in their elementary course of studies. Other grammatical features occasionally occur and reoccur with which the students may not be so familiar, but their use is made clear through context and reinforcement. This ensures that the reading as well as being enjoyable provides a continual learning situation for the students. Sentences are kept short – a maximum of two clauses in nearly all cases – and within sentences there is a balanced use of simple adverbial and adjectival phrases. Great care is taken with pronoun reference.

Vocabulary Control At Elementary Level there is a limited use of carefully controlled vocabulary (approximately 1,100 basic words). At the same time, students are given some opportunity to meet new or unfamiliar words in contexts where their meaning is obvious. The meaning of words introduced in this way is reinforced by repetition. Help is also given to the students in the form of vivid illustrations which are closely related to the text.

Some Guided Readers at Elementary Level

HEINEMANN GUIDED READERS
ELEMENTARY LEVEL

W. SOMERSET MAUGHAM

The Verger and Other Stories

Retold by

JOHN MILNE

Illustrated by

Elizabeth Grant

HEINEMANN EDUCATIONAL BOOKS
LONDON

Heinemann Educational Books Ltd
22 Bedford Square, London WC1B 3HH
LONDON EDINBURGH MELBOURNE AUCKLAND
HONG KONG SINGAPORE KUALA LUMPUR NEW DELHI
NAIROBI JOHANNESBURG PORTSMOUTH (NH) KINGSTON

ISBN 0 435 27018 4

'The Verger' and 'The String of Beads' were first
published in *Cosmopolitans* (1936), 'The Kite' and
'The Happy Couple' in *Creatures of Circumstance*
(1947) and 'Before the Party' in *The Casuarina Tree*
(1926) by William Heinemann

These retold versions for Heinemann Guided Readers
© John Milne 1975

These versions first published 1975
Reprinted 1976, 1978, 1980, 1982, 1986

Cover by Bill Heyes

Set in 11 pt Plantin

Printed and bound in Great Britain by
Richard Clay (The Chaucer Press) Ltd,
Bungay, Suffolk

Contents

A complete list of unsimplified books by W. Somerset Maugham can be found on page 42.

A String of Beads

Miss Robinson had always been poor. When her father died, she had no money. She got a job at the house of Mrs Livingstone – a rich woman with two young daughters. Miss Robinson's job was teaching Mrs Livingstone's daughters at home. She was their governess.

Miss Robinson lived in the house of Mrs Livingstone like a servant. But she was intelligent and well-educated. And sometimes she was asked to dinner when the Livingstones had visitors.

One evening, Mrs Livingstone invited some friends to dinner. She asked fourteen people. At the last moment, one of the guests was unable to come. Mrs Livingstone now had thirteen guests. But thirteen is an unlucky number and so she invited Miss Robinson.

The people at the dinner were all rich and important. Miss Robinson sat quietly and did not say anything. She was wearing an old dress of Mrs Livingstone's and she looked pretty. She was also wearing a string of pearls.

One of the guests at the dinner was Count Borselli – a rich and famous man. He knew everything about pearls and diamonds and other precious stones.

There was a young lady at dinner called Miss Lyngate. She, also, was wearing a string of pearls. She was very proud of her pearls and she asked Count Borselli to look at them.

'They're quite nice pearls,' said the Count.

This did not please Miss Lyngate. 'Quite nice' was not good enough for her. She had wanted the Count to say 'very nice' – 'very, very nice'.

'This string of pearls cost eight thousand pounds,' said Miss Lyngate.

'Yes, that's the correct price,' said Count Borselli. He spoke in an ordinary voice. But Miss Lyngate understood. The Count did not think that eight thousand pounds was a lot of money.

At that moment, Count Borselli pointed to Miss Robinson.

'*That* is a very nice string of pearls,' he said.

'Miss Robinson's pearls,' said Miss Lyngate. 'But she's Mrs Livingstone's governess!'

Miss Lyngate was now angry. Governesses were not rich people. A governess did not wear a valuable string of pearls.

'We're not talking about governesses,' replied the Count. 'We're talking about pearls. That string of pearls is worth more than fifty thousand pounds.'

Miss Lyngate was surprised and angry. She did not believe Count Borselli. He was mistaken. Governesses did *not* wear strings of pearls worth more than fifty thousand pounds.

'Miss Robinson,' she said in a loud voice. 'Do you know that you are wearing a very valuable string of pearls?'

Everyone stopped talking. They all listened to Miss Robinson's reply.

'I paid fifteen shillings for these beads,' said Miss Robinson quietly.

Miss Lyngate laughed.

'I knew that Count Borselli was wrong,' she said. 'He says that your pearls are worth fifty thousand pounds.'

Now everyone in the room was silent. Fifty thousand pounds! A governess with a string of pearls worth fifty thousand pounds! That was not possible. A woman with fifty thousand pounds was a very rich woman.

'But I bought these beads for fifteen shillings,' said Miss Robinson again. 'Count Borselli has made a mistake.'

'I do not make mistakes,' said the Count quietly. 'I know the value of pearls.'

At that moment something unusual happened. A servant came up to the table and spoke quietly to Miss Robinson. The governess looked surprised and her face went white.

'Excuse me, Mrs Livingstone,' she said. 'I must leave the table. Two men are waiting in the hall. They want to speak to me.'

Miss Robinson got up and left the table. When she was out of the room, everyone began to talk excitedly.

'She's a thief,' said someone. 'The two men are policemen. Miss Robinson has stolen the pearls. She will go to prison.'

'A thief in my house,' cried Mrs Livingstone. 'How terrible! What shall I do? What has she been teaching my daughters?'

Everyone started to talk at the same time. Suddenly there was silence. Miss Robinson had come back into the room. She looked much happier. She did not look like a thief.

Miss Robinson was not wearing her pearls. Instead, she had a string of pearls in her hand. She sat down at the table and passed the string of pearls over to Count Borselli.

'How much are these pearls worth?' she asked.

Count Borselli looked at the pearls for a few moments.

'Fifteen shillings,' he said.

'That's correct,' said Miss Robinson. 'These are my beads. They're worth fifteen shillings.'

'But what about the other string of pearls?' asked the Count. 'These are different.'

'That's correct,' replied Miss Robinson. 'My beads were broken and I took them to a shop a few days ago. When I went to get them, there was a mistake. The shop gave me the wrong string of pearls. That other string of pearls was worth fifty thousand pounds.'

Everyone laughed. It had all been a mistake.

'The men from the shop were very pleased to get the pearls back,' said Miss Robinson. 'They've given me a present of three hundred pounds.'

Again, everyone talked at the same time. Three hundred pounds was a lot of money for a governess.

Mrs Livingstone stopped everyone talking.

'What are you going to do with the three hundred pounds?' she asked loudly.

But she did not wait for a reply.

'You must put the money in a bank,' she said. 'You must keep it safely. You may need it one day.'

'I'm not going to put the money in a bank,' replied Miss Robinson proudly. 'All my life I've never had a holiday. Now I'm going to have a real holiday. I want to leave my work here at the end of the month. I'm going to the South of France.'

Mrs Livingstone looked at her angrily. A governess was a servant. Servants did not go on holiday to the South of France. And, also, governesses accepted the advice of their masters and mistresses.

'You can leave at the end of the month,' said Mrs Livingstone in an angry voice. 'But you need not come back again. There will be no job for you here.'

'I don't want to come back here,' replied Miss Robinson. And she got up quietly and left the room.

*

At the end of the month, Miss Robinson went on holiday to the South of France. Mrs Livingstone was not pleased. She hoped to hear bad news about Miss Robinson.

Six months later, Mrs Livingstone gave another dinner. Miss Lyngate, Count Borselli and other friends were there. They all remembered Miss Robinson. Someone started to talk about her.

'Miss Robinson will never come back here again,' said Mrs Livingstone in a loud voice.

'Miss Robinson will not want to come back,' said Count Borselli. 'Haven't you heard the news?'

'What news?' someone asked excitedly.

'I've just come from the South of France,' replied the Count. 'Everyone there is talking about Miss Robinson. But that's not her name now. She's a countess. She met a count in her hotel and married him soon afterwards. The count is a millionaire and she now lives with him in Paris. She'll never work as a governess again.'

'And all because of a mistake,' said Miss Lyngate. 'A cheap string of beads has made her a countess and a millionaire.'

The Verger

Mr Foreman owned ten shops in different parts of
London. All the shops sold the same things – cigars,
cigarettes, tobacco and pipes. The shops were always very
busy and Mr Foreman was a rich man.

But he had not always been rich. Albert Foreman's
parents had been very poor. They did not have enough
money to send Albert to school. Albert started work at the
age of ten. He was a servant in the house of a rich family.
He was young and he did all the dirty work.

Albert was a hard worker. He grew older and was given
more important jobs. Albert was always clean and tidy. He
was well dressed and looked respectable. At the age of
twenty, Albert Foreman was the head servant in the house
of a rich man.

Albert married at the age of twenty-two. His wife was
also a working woman. She had been a servant in the same
house as Albert.

Then Albert got a new job. He became the verger of
St Peter's Church. St Peter's was in Neville Square, in the
centre of the richest part of London. Rich and important
people lived in the houses nearby. They were taken to
St Peter's as babies and given names. They were married
in St Peter's and they were buried near St Peter's when
they died.

The verger was present at all these important times. He
stood near the door wearing a long black robe. Also, he
kept the church clean and tidy.

The people at St Peter's were pleased with Mr Foreman.
He worked there for sixteen years. During this time, there
was no trouble. The old vicar liked and trusted Mr
Foreman. He knew that Albert was not able to read or
write. But this did not matter. Albert Foreman looked
important and respectable and he kept the church clean.

That was enough.

But in life nothing lasts for ever. The vicar grew older. At last, he was no longer able to do the work. He had to leave St Peter's and go and live in the country. A new vicar came to St Peter's. He was young and wanted to change many things.

Mr Foreman did not like the new vicar. But he obeyed him. Mr Foreman did things the new way.

'Don't walk like that,' said the new vicar. 'Walk like this.'

'Don't stand like that,' said the new vicar. 'Stand like this.'

Albert Foreman had to change everything. But there was one thing which did not change. Albert was not able to read or write. At last, the new vicar heard about this.

One day, after an important wedding, the young vicar spoke to Albert.

'How long have you been verger at St Peter's?' he asked.

'Sixteen years, sir,' replied Albert.

'You have been verger for sixteen years,' said the vicar, 'and you cannot read or write?'

'That's true,' replied Albert. 'I was born in a poor family. My parents weren't able to send me to school. I never learned to read or to write?'

'But this is an important church,' said the vicar. 'The verger of St Peter's must be able to read and write.'

'You've asked me to change many things,' replied Albert. 'I've done my best to please you. But I can't learn to read and write. I'm getting older now. It's too late for me to learn such things.'

'You must learn to read and write,' said the vicar, 'or you cannot be verger at St Peter's.'

Albert Foreman was a proud man. He had tried to

please the new vicar. He had done enough.

'I'll leave at the end of this month,' Albert told the vicar. 'You must find a new verger. Find another man and I'll teach him his job.'

Albert said goodnight politely and left the church. He was not angry, but he felt sad. He started to walk home.

'What will my wife say?' Albert asked himself. 'She'll be angry and worried. I must find a new job, but it won't be easy.'

*

Albert did not smoke much, but now he wanted a cigarette.

'I must buy a packet of cigarettes,' he said to himself. 'I'll smoke a cigarette and I'll feel better.'

Albert started to look for a cigarette shop. He turned into a long street where there were many shops. There were bakers shops and butchers shops. There were shoe shops and hat shops. But there were no shops which sold tobacco or cigarettes.

Albert walked all the way home, but he did not find a cigarette shop.

'I've lost my job,' he told his wife when he got home.

'You've lost your job!' she said in surprise. 'Why?'

'The new vicar wants a verger who can read and write,' replied Albert.

'But what are you going to do?' asked Albert's wife. 'You're over forty now. You won't find a new job easily.'

'I've an idea,' said Albert. 'On my way home, I wanted to smoke a cigarette, but there wasn't a cigarette shop. How many other people have wanted a cigarette in this part of London?'

'A lot of people,' replied his wife.

WHITES
FAMILY
GROCER
ON
G. F.
PLAYERS

'And they can't buy them here,' said Albert. 'Now, how much money have we saved?'

Albert and his wife had always been careful. They had saved up a little money every week.

'We have enough,' said Albert, when they had counted the money.

'Enough for what?' asked his wife.

'To open a cigarette shop,' Albert replied.

At the end of the month, Albert Foreman left St Peter's for ever. He opened a shop and sold cigarettes.

Many people came into his shop because it was the only one in the street. He began to sell other things. But they were all things for smokers. He sold tobacco for pipes. He sold cigars and matches. And every week the shop became busier.

*

After a year, Albert's shop was making a lot of money. Then Albert had another idea.

'Why don't we open another shop?' he said to his wife.

His wife agreed with him.

Albert Foreman walked round London. At last he found a long, busy street with no cigarette shop. Albert opened another shop in that street. A young man worked in the shop for him. The shop soon became very busy.

Albert did the same thing again and again. After ten years, he owned ten cigarette shops. All of them were very busy and every week Albert put more and more money into the bank.

When Albert was in the bank one day, a bank clerk spoke to him.

'Excuse me, Mr Foreman,' said the clerk. 'The manager wants to speak to you. Can you see him?'

'Of course,' replied Albert and he went into the manager's office.

The manager wanted to talk to Albert about his money.

'You have a lot of money in the bank now,' said the manager.

'Yes, I know,' replied Albert. 'It's safe in the bank. I don't need the money. The money is safer here.'

'Of course your money is safe in our bank,' said the manager. 'But a bank doesn't pay much interest. You can buy shares in business and make more money.'

'I don't know anything about things like that,' replied Albert. 'I'll need help.'

'But I'll help you,' said the manager.

He gave Mr Foreman a piece of paper with lots of writing on it.

'You must sign here,' said the manager. 'Then I can do everything else for you.'

Albert picked up a pen and put a large cross at the bottom of the paper.

'But why have you made this mark?' asked the manager. 'Why didn't you sign it with your name?'

'Because I can't read or write,' replied Albert simply.

The manager sat back in his seat.

'You're a rich man, Mr Foreman,' said the manager. 'And yet you cannot read or write. If you could read and write, you would be a millionaire.'

Albert Foreman laughed loudly. The manager was surprised.

'I'm rich *because* I cannot read or write,' said Albert smiling. 'If I could read and write, I would be poor. I would still be verger at St Peter's Church in Neville Square.'

The Kite

Herbert Sunbury was given his first kite when he was a young boy. Every Sunday, he went to a nearby park with his mother and father. The three of them walked to a hill in the middle of the park and flew their kite. That was how the kite flying began.

Herbert left school when he was fourteen. He got a good job in an office. He was a clerk like his father. He was not paid much, but it was a regular job.

The family had a little party for Herbert's twenty-first birthday. Herbert was given a present – a big, new kite. After the party, Herbert went to bed and his mother and father sat talking.

'He's not a boy any more,' said Mr Sunbury. 'He's a man now. He'll want to get married soon.'

'Get married!' said Mrs Sunbury in surprise. 'Why? He's happy here at home with us.'

Mr Sunbury did not reply. He never argued with his wife.

Two years passed and nothing changed. Herbert and Mr Sunbury went to work every morning. They came back together in the evening and sat at home. At weekends, they went to the park with Mrs Sunbury and flew their kite.

One Saturday evening, there was a change. They had all been out in the park as usual and they were sitting at tea.

'Can I bring a girl home tomorrow, mother?' Herbert suddenly asked.

'A girl!' said Mrs Sunbury in surprise. 'Who is she? Where did you meet her?'

Herbert had met the girl at the cinema. He sometimes

went there on a Friday evening. Her name was Betty Bevan.

Betty came for tea the next day, but her visit was not a success. Mrs Sunbury did not like Betty and Betty did not like Mrs Sunbury.

'Never bring that girl back to this house,' said Mrs Sunbury after the visit. 'You're a fool to go out with her.'

'I'm going to marry her,' said Herbert angrily.

'You're a fool,' cried his mother. 'You're a fool.'

They did not speak about Betty again for some months. But Herbert continued to meet her. He went out two or three evenings every week. He met Betty and usually they went to the cinema.

Late one evening, Herbert came back from the cinema. His mother was just going to bed.

'Mother,' he said. 'Betty and I are getting married.'

'You can do what you like,' shouted his mother. 'But don't bring that girl back to this house. I never want to see her again.'

*

A week later, Herbert and Betty got married. Mr and Mrs Sunbury did not go to the wedding. Herbert lived with Betty and he did not see his mother again for some time. He still met his father on his way to work every morning. And he often spoke to him.

One morning Mr Sunbury looked up at the sky.

'It's good weather for kite flying,' he said.

'Do you and mother still fly the kite?' asked Herbert.

'Of course,' replied his father. 'We go to the park every weekend as usual. Don't you fly a kite yourself? You always liked flying a kite.'

16

'I wanted to get one,' replied Herbert. 'But Betty
doesn't like kites. She says they're only for children.
Also, kites cost a lot of money. We need all our money.
We've got some nice furniture, but I have to pay for it
every month.'

Six months passed and Mr and Mrs Sunbury still went
to the park. One Sunday afternoon, Mrs Sunbury spoke
quietly to her husband.

'Look over there,' she said. 'Herbert is watching us.'

Mrs Sunbury was happy to see her son, but she did not
speak to him. Herbert came every Sunday and watched
them.

One Sunday, Mr and Mrs Sunbury brought a new kite.
It was the biggest and best kite in the park. The wind was
strong and the kite flew high in the sky. A young man
wanted to help them. But Herbert saw this and ran up
quickly.

'I'll help you,' he cried. 'We don't want strangers
touching our kite.'

After that, Herbert flew the new kite with his mother
and father every Sunday. One day, while Herbert was
flying the kite, his mother spoke to him.

'Betty's here,' she said.

'Betty?' asked Herbert. 'Where?'

'Behind those trees,' replied his mother. 'She's spying on
you.'

When Herbert got back home that evening, Betty was
waiting for him.

'So that's where you've been on Sunday afternoons,' she
shouted. 'You look like a small boy with that kite. You look
foolish.'

'I don't care,' replied Herbert.

'It's your mother's plan,' said Betty. 'She wants to take

you away from me.'

The following Sunday, Herbert got ready to go to the park.

'Where are you going?' asked Betty.

'To the park,' Herbert replied. 'I'm going to fly the kite with my mother and father.'

'You're not,' cried Betty. 'I'm not going to let you.'

She tried to stop him, but Herbert pushed past her.

Herbert came back later that afternoon and Betty was waiting for him.

'Your bag's packed,' she told him.

'What do you mean?' he asked.

'You're not staying here,' she explained. 'You like kites better than you like me. You can go back to them.'

*

That was the way it happened. Herbert went and lived with his mother and father. He was comfortable at home with them. The food was good and Herbert felt happy.

'I'm never going back to Betty,' he told his mother.

'She'll try to get you back,' was her reply.

Mrs Sunbury was right. Betty came round to see Herbert. But Herbert did not want to see her. Mrs Sunbury spoke to Betty at the door.

'Herbert will send you money every week,' she told Betty. 'He'll pay for the furniture. Now leave him alone.'

Then she shut the door. Betty knocked again and again. Then she banged at the windows. But Mrs Sunbury did not open the door and after some time Betty went away.

The next Sunday, Herbert went to church with his mother and father in the morning. In the afternoon, he went to get the kite. Because it was so big, they kept the

kite in a shed behind the house. Herbert found the door of the shed open. The kite – the big new kite – was broken to pieces.

'She's broken the kite,' shouted Herbert, running back into the house.

The three of them looked at each other in silence. They all thought that Betty had broken it. But Mr Sunbury was not sure.

'We don't know that it was Betty,' he said. 'There are other people in the park who are jealous of our kite.'

'I'll go and ask her,' said Herbert. 'I'll kill her for this.'

'No, you won't,' said his mother. 'You'll hit her and be sent to prison. Your father will go and speak to Betty.'

Mr Sunbury left and returned an hour later.

'Betty did it,' he told them. 'And she's happy about it.'

'That's the end of the money,' shouted Herbert. 'She'll get no more money from me.'

'What about the furniture?' asked Mrs Sunbury.

'I'll not pay for that,' said Herbert. 'They can take the furniture away. I don't want it.'

Herbert did not pay Betty any more money. She waited for him in the street and started shouting. She came round to their house and threw stones at the windows.

'Don't worry,' said Mrs Sunbury. 'She'll leave us alone soon.'

But Mrs Sunbury was wrong. Betty did not leave Herbert alone. She took him to court. And the magistrate ordered him to pay Betty one pound every week.

'I won't pay,' Herbert told the magistrate. 'She broke our kite. I'll never forgive her.'

'Then you'll go to prison,' said the magistrate.

Herbert did not pay and Betty again took him to court.

'You're a foolish young man,' said the magistrate. 'Pay

this money before the end of the week, or you will go to prison.'

Herbert did not pay and went to prison. He never forgave Betty for breaking the kite.

'He loved that kite more than he loved me,' said Betty.

Perhaps she was right.

Before the Party

It was a beautiful Saturday afternoon in June and the Skinners were going to a party. The party began at four o'clock, but Mrs Skinner was ready at two. She was always early.

The Bishop of Hong Kong was on a visit to England. He was going to the party. Mrs Skinner wanted to meet the Bishop. She wanted to talk to him about Harold.

Her daughter, Millicent, had married Harold eight years ago. After her marriage, Millicent had gone to the Far East with Harold. She had lived there until Harold's death a few months ago. Millicent and Harold had often met the Bishop in the Far East.

'Poor Harold,' thought Mrs Skinner, looking round the room. 'Poor Harold.'

Before his death, Harold had often sent presents from the Far East. Silver dishes and ornaments stood on tables and shelves. Mrs Skinner looked up at some large knives and swords on the walls. Harold had sent them, too.

Mrs Skinner looked at the piano. There had always been a photograph of Harold on the piano. The photograph was no longer there.

Mrs Skinner turned to the other person in the room. It was her second daughter, Kathleen.

'Where's the photograph of Harold?' asked Mrs Skinner.

Kathleen was busy writing letters.

'Someone's taken it away,' she said. Kathleen did not look up from her writing.

'Perhaps Millicent took it to her bedroom,' said Mrs Skinner.

'I don't think so,' replied Kathleen. 'Millicent doesn't have any photographs of Harold in her bedroom.'

This was true. Millicent had been very strange since her return from the Far East. She never spoke about Harold or his death. She often sat for hours and said nothing.

'Harold died of an illness,' Millicent had told her family. 'He died suddenly. I was away at the time. He was dead when I got back.'

She never said any more.

Mrs Skinner looked again at Kathleen. She was also ready for the party.

'You're dressed early,' said Mrs Skinner.

'Yes,' replied Kathleen. 'I want to talk to Millicent.'

Kathleen did not say any more. She carried on writing. Mrs Skinner looked out into the garden. Millicent's daughter, Joan, was playing there by herself. Joan had been born two years before Harold's death.

'She's a strange child,' thought Mrs Skinner. 'She's always playing by herself.'

At that moment, Mrs Skinner's husband came into the room. He was a small, tidy man. Mr Skinner was a lawyer and he had an office in London.

'Is Millicent ready?' asked Mrs Skinner.

'There's plenty of time,' replied Mr Skinner. 'We don't want to arrive at the party until four o'clock. And it's only two now.'

At last the door opened and Millicent came in. She was dressed completely in black.

*

When Millicent came into the room, Kathleen stopped writing. She looked at her sister for a moment. Then she spoke.

'I met Gladys Heywood this morning,' Kathleen began.

Gladys Heywood was the vicar's daughter. The Bishop of Hong Kong was staying with the vicar.

Millicent said nothing. She was not listening to Kathleen. Millicent was looking out of the window. She had seen Joan in the garden.

'Will Joan have her tea alone?' Millicent asked Mrs Skinner.

'No,' Mrs Skinner replied. 'She'll have tea with the servants.'

Millicent looked out of the window and said nothing.

'She told me something very strange,' Kathleen continued.

'Who did?' asked Millicent.

'Gladys Heywood, of course,' replied Kathleen. 'I met her this morning. The Bishop has told her about Harold's death.'

Mrs Skinner looked at her two daughters. Kathleen's words had made her curious.

'What about Harold's death?' she asked.

'Harold did not die of fever,' said Kathleen. 'Harold

killed himself.'

Mrs Skinner gave a cry. Her husband began to listen. Millicent stood silently, looking out of the window.

'Is this true, Millicent?' asked Mrs Skinner.

'Yes, it's true,' Millicent replied simply.

'How terrible!' cried Mrs Skinner. 'Why didn't you tell us the truth?'

'I didn't tell anybody,' replied Millicent.

'But you must tell us the truth,' said Kathleen.

'Yes,' added Mrs Skinner. 'You must tell us everything.'

'It's always best to tell the truth,' said Mr Skinner.

'The truth?' asked Millicent with a strange smile. 'Do you want the truth?'

'Yes,' they replied. And they all waited.

Millicent began her story.

*

'Harold was very drunk when he died,' Millicent began.

'Drunk?' said Mrs Skinner in surprise. 'Did Harold drink?'

'All the time,' replied Millicent quietly.

'How terrible!' cried Mrs Skinner. 'How did it all begin?'

'I first met Harold in this house,' replied Millicent. 'He did not drink then.'

That was true. Harold had been in England on holiday and he never drank then. He had stayed at a house in the village. Mr and Mrs Skinner had met him and invited him to their home. That was how Millicent had met him. A friendship had started between her and Harold. Mrs Skinner had hoped for this. Perhaps she had planned it.

'I didn't love Harold when I married him,' continued Millicent.

'Don't say such things,' said her mother.

'Keep quiet,' said Mr Skinner, giving his wife a strange look. He wanted to hear his daughter's story.

'I was twenty-seven when I met Harold,' continued Millicent. 'He was forty-four. I liked him, but I didn't love him. When he asked me to marry him, I agreed.

'We got married quickly. We went to Venice for two weeks. Then we sailed to the Far East.

'First we went to Kuala Solor, the chief town in Harold's district. The English people there were nice to me. But I noticed something strange. When Harold was offered a drink, he always refused. Then everybody laughed. I didn't know why.

'After a few days, we left Kuala Solor. We travelled up the river to Harold's village. It was beautiful in the jungle, but it was very lonely. There was one other Englishman in in the village – a young man called Simpson. He was Harold's assistant.

'Everything went well for the first year. I was happy in my new life and Harold worked hard. He was good at his job and all the people liked him.'

'He wasn't drinking then?' asked Kathleen.

'No,' replied Millicent. 'He didn't drink at all in that first year. Then two English visitors arrived. They stayed with us for a few days. We all enjoyed meeting the strangers. But Harold kept giving them whisky. They all became very drunk. Later that night, Harold was sick. That was the beginning.

'Harold didn't drink again for some months. Then he caught a fever. He went back to work after two weeks, but he was strange. He came home from the office in the

evening with red eyes. His hands were often shaking.

'I was very worried. And Simpson was worried, too. I tried to talk to Simpson. At first he kept away from me. But at last he told me everything. Harold had a bottle of whisky in the office. He was drinking every day.

'I went to the office and found Harold. He was very drunk. We had a quarrel and I cried. I told him that I was going to have a baby. This news made him happy and he promised never to drink again.

'Harold stopped drinking and I was happy again. Soon it was time for the baby to be born. I had to go to Kuala Solor because there was no doctor or nurse in our village.

'At Kuala Solor, I learned the truth about Harold. He had never loved me. He had married me because he needed help. He wanted to stop drinking.

'When Joan was born, I returned to our village. Harold was waiting for me by the river. He was not standing properly. He had been drinking. That night, we had a quarrel.

'I wanted to leave him and come back to England. This frightened Harold. He did not want to lose the baby or me. He promised never to drink again.

'Harold didn't drink again for two years. They were happy years for me. Slowly I began to fall in love with him. When he wasn't drinking, he was a good man and he loved his daughter, Joan.

'But the village wasn't a healthy place. Joan became ill. I had to take her down the river to the sea. The air was fresh there and she soon became better. I was away from Harold for about four weeks.

'During that time, I thought a lot about Harold. I was now really in love with him. He had fought against drink and he had won.

'I returned to our village after the four weeks. I was happy to be back. But when I arrived, Harold wasn't waiting for me. This was unusual.

'I went up to the house to look for him. It was strangely quiet. Joan went to the garden with the maid and I looked for Harold. I found him in the bedroom.'

Millicent stopped speaking. She was remembering the scene. Mr and Mrs Skinner and Kathleen waited in silence. Then Millicent continued.

'Harold was lying in bed,' she said. 'There was a bottle of whisky on the table beside the bed. He was completely drunk.'

'How terrible . . . .,' Mrs Skinner began to say. But her husband stopped her immediately.

'There was a large knife on the table,' Millicent continued. 'It was like that knife there.'

Millicent pointed to the wall. Mr and Mrs Skinner and Kathleen turned and looked. Millicent was pointing at a long, large knife on the wall.

'The next moment,' said Millicent, 'Harold was lying on the bed with his throat cut. The knife was lying beside him. It was covered with blood.'

*

There was silence. Then Mrs Skinner spoke.

'But how did Harold kill himself?' Mrs Skinner asked. 'You've just told us that he was completely drunk.'

'He didn't kill himself,' replied Millicent quietly. 'I killed him. Then I called out for the servants. They came quickly and someone went for Simpson. Everyone thought that Harold had killed himself. I didn't say anything.'

Her mother, father and sister were silent with horror. At last Mrs Skinner spoke.

'How terrible!' she said again. 'How terrible!'

'Why have you told me this?' cried Mr Skinner. 'I'm a lawyer. I must tell the police.'

'You can't tell the police,' said Millicent. 'The murderer is your own daughter.'

'Oh, why have you told us?' said Kathleen. 'Why have you told us?'

'You asked me to,' replied Millicent. 'You wanted to know the truth.'

The three were silent. From time to time, they looked at the large knife on the wall. Then Millicent spoke again.

'It's time to go to the party,' she said.

'The party!' cried Mrs Skinner. 'We can't go to the party.'

'We must,' replied Millicent. 'The Bishop is waiting for us. He'll want to talk about Harold.'

There was a noise of a car at the front door.

'But how can I speak to the Bishop?' asked Mrs Skinner.

'There's no danger,' said Millicent. 'No one will ever find out. It will be our secret.'

'Oh, why did you tell us the truth?' said Mrs Skinner, as she went down the steps to the car. 'Why? Why?'

Then they all got into the car and drove off to the party.

The Happy Couple

I did not know Judge Landon very well. He was a
famous judge. I had met him a few times, but we were
not really friends.

I was surprised, then, when I got a telegram from
Landon. His telegram was short:

Going to Italy for a holiday. Can I stay with you for a
few days?   Landon.

At that time, I was living in the South of France. I had a
villa on the Mediterranean coast near the Italian border.
My reply was shorter:

Glad to see you. Come any time.

Maugham.

Landon arrived a week later.
I did not know how to amuse Judge Landon. And so,
on the evening of his arrival, I invited Miss Gray to
dinner. Miss Gray was an Englishwoman who lived in a
villa nearby.
She was a cheerful woman and a good talker. She
amused the Judge and I was happy. After dinner, she
invited us both to lunch the following day.
We thanked her for the invitation and she got up to
leave.
'Oh – and perhaps you'll meet my new neighbours,' said
Miss Gray. 'Their name is Craig. They're such a happy
couple and they have a beautiful baby. I'll invite them to
lunch tomorrow.'

*

The next day, I drove Judge Landon to Miss Gray's
villa. It was a beautiful day. The sun was warm, but there
was a cool breeze blowing in from the sea. English people
live in the South of France because of such weather.

We arrived at Miss Gray's at one o'clock. We were both
hungry and ready for lunch.

'The Craigs are coming,' Miss Gray said as soon as we
arrived. 'I asked them to come at one.'

But the Craigs did not arrive until half-past one.

'We had to wait until the baby fell asleep,' they
explained.

Miss Gray introduced the Craigs to the Judge. It was a
strange introduction. Judge Landon put on his spectacles
and looked carefully at the Craigs. He did not shake hands.
He turned and looked out of the window.

Both the Craigs looked surprised.

'What a rude man he is!' I thought to myself. 'No
wonder they look surprised.'

The maid brought in lunch and we all sat down at the
table. The Judge again looked carefully at Mr and Mrs
Craig. Suddenly he spoke.

'Haven't we met somewhere before?'

Mr Craig looked down at the table and said nothing. It
was his wife who replied.

'I don't think so,' she said. 'Of course, we have heard of
you. Everybody has read about Judge Landon in the
newspapers.'

Judge Landon sat silently and ate his meal.

Miss Gray and I tried to talk to the Craigs. But it was
difficult. They did not speak very much. They only
wanted to talk about the baby.

Suddenly Mr Craig dropped his fork on to his plate. His
face turned white. He stood up and then fell to the floor.

Mrs Craig jumped up and gave a frightened shout. I bent down and looked at him. His eyes were closed and he was breathing deeply.

'He's fainted,' I said.

'We must send for a doctor,' said Miss Gray.

'No, no,' said Mrs Craig, kneeling down beside her husband. 'He'll be all right in a moment or two.'

Judge Landon had not moved. He was sitting at the table and still eating his lunch.

'What a rude, cruel man, he is,' I thought.

After a few minutes, Craig slowly opened his eyes and his wife helped him to his feet.

'I'll take him home,' said Mrs Craig. 'Our villa is not far away.'

The Craigs left and Miss Gray and I sat down again at the table.

'Do you think he'll be all right?' asked Miss Gray.

'Yes, I'm sure he'll be all right,' I replied.

Judge Landon sat quietly drinking his coffee. He did not listen to our conversation.

'He doesn't like the Craigs,' I thought. 'He's not interested in them at all. What a rude man!'

Later in the afternoon, we drove back to my villa. It had not been a pleasant lunch party.

*

The next day, the Judge and I were having lunch together. The telephone rang. It was Miss Gray.

'Something strange has happened,' she said excitedly.

'Oh – yes,' I replied. 'What?'

'The Craigs have gone away.'

'Gone away?' I asked. 'What's strange about that?'

'They've taken everything with them,' she replied.

'That *is* strange,' I said. 'I wonder why they left so suddenly.'

Miss Gray did not know why. No one did.

I went back to the Judge. He had finished lunch and the maid had brought coffee. I told him about Miss Gray's telephone call.

'So, the "happy couple" have run away,' he said quietly.

'You're surprised?' I said.

'No – not at all,' the judge replied. 'I expected it.'

'Expected it?' I asked in surprise. 'Do you know something about the Craigs.'

'I'll tell you a story,' said the Judge. 'It's an interesting story. You'll enjoy it.'

Judge Landon made himself comfortable. I gave him a glass of brandy and he began his story.

*

'Do you remember the Wingford murder?' he asked me.

'No.'

'Perhaps you weren't in England at the time,' the Judge continued. 'The Wingford murder caused a lot of excitement. It was in the newspapers every day.'

'Miss Wingford was a rich, old lady. She was not married and lived in the country with a companion. Miss Wingford was old, but she was healthy. When she died suddenly, everyone was surprised.

'Her doctor was a man called Brandon. Dr Brandon signed the death certificate. And, a few days later, Miss Wingford was buried.

'The trouble started after the funeral. Miss Wingford

left all her money to her companion. She left nothing to
her relatives or maids.

'One of the maids had worked for Miss Wingford for
thirty years. Miss Wingford had promised this maid some
money. But the maid had been left nothing and she began
to make trouble. She said that someone had poisoned
Miss Wingford.

'The police heard these stories and they decided to
dig up Miss Wingford's body. The body was full of
poison. The maid's story seemed to be true. Someone had
murdered Miss Wingford.

'A detective came down from London and arrested Miss
Starling.'

'Miss Starling?' I asked. 'Who was she?'

'Miss Starling was Miss Wingford's companion,' replied
the Judge. 'She was the woman who got all the money.

'The detective discovered a lot of things. Miss Starling
and Dr Brandon had been friends for a long time. They
were going to get married after Miss Wingford's death.'

'Did the police arrest both of them?' I asked.

'That's right,' replied Judge Landon. 'And I was the
judge at their trial.'

'And Miss Starling and Dr Brandon were found guilty
of murder?' I asked Judge Landon.

'Strange things happen at trials,' replied the Judge. 'You
never know what a jury will decide. Twelve ordinary men
and women say that a person is guilty or not guilty. A
judge can only advise the jury.'

'But weren't they guilty?' I said.

'Yes,' said Judge Landon. 'I was sure that they were
guilty. But it is the jury who decides. Miss Starling and
Dr Brandon were found not guilty. The couple left the
court together.'

'An interesting story,' I said. 'But why have you told me this? You must have some reason.'

'I saw Miss Starling and Dr Brandon again yesterday,' replied the Judge.

'Yesterday?' I said in surprise. 'Where?'

'At Miss Gray's,' was the reply. 'Miss Starling and Dr Brandon are married now. They have changed their name to Craig. And Miss Gray calls them "the happy couple"!'

Points for Understanding

A String of Beads
1. What does a governess do?
2. Why did Mrs Livingstone invite Miss Robinson to dinner?
3. Was Count Borselli right or wrong about the value of Miss Robinson's pearls?
4. How was Miss Robinson able to go for a holiday to France?
5. What happened to Miss Robinson in the South of France?

The Verger
1. Was Albert Foreman good at his job as verger?
2. Why did he lose his job at St Peter's church?
3. What gave Albert the idea of opening a cigarette shop?
4. How did Albert sign his name in the bank?
5. Why had Albert become a rich man?

The Kite
1 Why did Mr and Mrs Sunbury not go to Herbert's wedding?
2. How did Herbert's life change after his marriage?
3. Why did Betty ask Herbert to leave?
4. Why did Herbert stop paying for the furniture?
5. Why did Herbert go to prison?
6. Betty said: 'Herbert loves the kite more than he loves me.'
   Was she right or wrong?

Before the Party
1. Why did Mrs Skinner want to meet the Bishop of Hong
   Kong?
2. What had Millicent told her family about Harold's death?
3. What did Gladys Heywood tell Kathleen?
4. Everyone laughed at Kuala Solor when Harold refused a
   drink. Why?
5. When did Millicent begin to love Harold?
6. How had Harold died?

The Happy Couple
1. When Maugham got a telegram from Judge Landon, he was
   surprised. Why?
2. What question did Judge Landon ask the Craigs at the
   lunch party?
3. What did the Judge do when Mr Craig fainted?
4. Why did Miss Gray telephone Maugham?
5. Judge Landon believed that Miss Starling and Dr Brandon
   were guilty. Why were they not sent to prison?
6. Who were 'the happy couple'?

Books by W Somerset Maugham (unsimplified)

LIZA OF LAMBETH
MRS CRADDOCK
THE MAGICIAN
OF HUMAN BONDAGE
THE MOON AND SIXPENCE
THE TREMBLING OF A LEAF
ON A CHINESE SCREEN
THE PAINTED VEIL
THE CASUARINA TREE
ASHENDEN
THE GENTLEMAN IN THE PARLOUR
CAKES AND ALE
FIRST PERSON SINGULAR
THE NARROW CORNER
AH KING
DON FERNANDO
COSMOPOLITANS
THEATRE
THE SUMMING UP
CHRISTMAS HOLIDAY
BOOKS AND YOU
THE MIXTURE AS BEFORE
UP AT THE VILLA
STRICTLY PERSONAL
THE RAZOR'S EDGE
THEN AND NOW
CREATURES OF CIRCUMSTANCE
CATALINA
HERE AND THERE *(Collection of Short Stories)*
QUARTET *(Four Short Stories with Film Scripts)*
A WRITER'S NOTEBOOK
TRIO *(Three Short Stories with Film Scripts)*
THE COMPLETE SHORT STORIES (3 Vols.)
ENCORE *(Three Short Stories with Film Scripts)*
THE VAGRANT MOOD
THE COLLECTED PLAYS *(3 vols.)*
THE SELECTED NOVELS *(3 vols.)*
THE PARTIAL VIEW
TEN NOVELS AND THEIR AUTHORS
THE TRAVEL BOOKS